ExtraCurricular Press
327 Guerrero Street
San Francisco, CA 94103
extracurricularpress.com

Third printing June 2018

Agenda

0   Getting started

1   How to give a presentation

2   How to write an email

3   How to get promoted

Introduction

How to write an email was first published in December 2015. The original printing sold out in just 29 days as I took my message to companies big and small in New York City, San Francisco, Los Angeles, Iowa City and Tokyo.

And while I started the book tour with a belief that my mission was to teach people how to maximize their effort in the corporate work setting, I came to realize my true passion—the underlying truth of this book—is an obsession with efficiency and the power of over-communication.

Over the past 15 years I've been the youngest executive at Gap Inc., Levi's and UNIQLO, running billion-dollar businesses before the age of 31—and yet I've rarely worked past 5pm or checked my email on the weekend. I never looked the part of a company man and I ruffled plenty of feathers along the way. I've made my share of rookie mistakes—some of them small, some of them serious—but the secret to my success was that I got a few fundamentals right.

Part survival guide, part corporate myth-buster, *How to write an email* shows you the basic behaviors that will set you apart from your peers and help you get credit for all the work you do. Whether you work at a Fortune 500 company or the latest tech start-up, the simple, actionable steps highlighted in this book will change the way you communicate forever. (My wife made me stop short of a money-back guarantee).

How to write an email is aimed at new employees but it's useful for anyone who wants to be great at what they do.

0/
Getting
started

Before you open your mouth to talk or open an email to type, there are two fundamentals you must absolutely commit yourself to when you are first getting started in corporate America. Be early. Be accurate.

When you are new to a job you don't know anything. In fact, every single person in the office knows more than you do. They know how to set up their computer to the printer. They know a bunch of acronyms that sound really important. They know the best places to go for lunch.

If you're anything like me, when you first start your new job you will have a vague sense that you will never be able to pick up all the phrases and codes that are dropped constantly into every conversation. You'll walk around the first few weeks thinking that everyone is smarter than you are and you should probably just give up.

Well, I'm here to tell you to set all of these doubts aside because none of that matters. Being accurate and being early—that is all that matters.

Be accurate

The first thing you need to do as a new employee is build trust. More important than convincing people you're smart—remember you don't know anything yet—is convincing people that they can trust you. The best way to do this—the easy way to do this—is to make sure that everything you do is accurate. Nothing undermines trust like delivering inaccurate information.

You're probably eager to prove yourself but when you're starting out it's far better to be a bit slower and more accurate than a bit faster and wrong. Understand this. Live this.

When you're doing work in Excel, double-check the formulas. When you send a document make sure it's formatted to print on one page—not 37 pages with one sentence on each. When you're sending information with dates, double-check the schedule. Even one mistake among a hundred data points is one too many.

Of course mistakes are going to happen, but you can at least eliminate all the dumb ones.

Be early

There are three key elements to being early:

- Get to work early

- Turn in your work early

- Leave early

Get to work early

I don't care if you aren't a morning person. Figure it out. Showing up to work at the same time as everyone else is a ticket to mediocrity—and a slow promotion.

Get to work one hour before everyone else. One hour of work in peace and quiet is worth three hours in the office when other people are there, meetings are happening, everyone's talking and you're distracted. Adding three hours of productive time is a very good thing when it only costs you one hour.

Here's what you can accomplish in one extra hour:

- Read and reply to all emails that are outstanding

- Review your calendar and prepare for how the day will go

- Have time for any last-minute prep

- Review your to-do list

- Send out emails reminding people what you need from them

- Read your favorite website undisturbed (for me it's grant-land.com)

There's another upshot to getting to work early that's less tangible but just as important: you begin to build the perception that you are a top performer.

Look around at the other people that show up early. I bet you they are the most successful people in the company. This means something. It also means something if these people are seeing you at work early. As LeBron James once tweeted: *Game recognizes game.*

Watch what happens to people who show up to work "on time." Often they get pulled into an unexpected meeting before they even have a chance to check their email. Then walking down the hall their boss asks if they've seen the latest on whatever project is on tap. Their reply? *No, I haven't had a chance to check it yet.* Oops—now they look like a dope who isn't on top of their business.

Can you hear that? That's the sound of their blinker as they unexpectedly drift into the slow lane of the promotion super highway.

Turn in your work early

To most people, turning in an assignment on time means doing a good job. These same people also think that turning in an assignment an hour early is an above target performance. They're wrong.

Always aim to deliver your work 24 hours in advance of a deadline.

An average boss is going to tell the team that they need the report by end of day Thursday. As you'll see later, this is already a mistake by the boss since EOD means something different to every person in the office.

If your boss asks for something by EOD Thursday, you should send it to them by 5pm on Wednesday. Why 5pm? Because you want to catch your boss before they leave on Wednesday. You want to get credit for delivering the work early and it's much more impressive to deliver the day before rather than the morning of.

Also, it's likely your boss is already thinking about the deadline and getting nervous about whether everyone on the team will hit it. By sending the report 24 hours in advance you've pre-empted their concern. You've also given them a nice reminder that everyone else hasn't delivered the information yet. Typically upon receiving your report they will thank you—and then send a reminder to everyone else on the team that the report is due EOD the next day.

You want to avoid being the recipient of one of these reminder emails at all costs—the result of which is that even if you deliver the report on time, the boss' experience of the deadline is that they had to remind you about it instead of you delivering it without being asked. This makes a big difference in the perception of your reliability and in developing a reputation as a go-to person.

OK, but sometimes you can't deliver the report 24 hours in advance. What then?

Even in these instances I recommend that you send an email to your boss 24 hours in advance (before 5pm while they're still at work) giving them the status update and reassuring them of your progress:

I'm working on it, I just need to finalize a few details—but I will send to you by X hour tomorrow.

This way, you're controlling the flow of communication.

Think of your performance this way:

• A = 24 hours in advance

• B = Same day as deadline

• C = At the deadline (5pm on an EOD deadline)

• D = EOD on an EOD deadline (after 7pm)

• F = Missed the deadline and gave no warning

An important note:

You can miss the deadline and still get an A. Here is how: you must give at least 48 hours notice that you're going to miss the deadline, and you must provide a new deadline proposal and a summary reason why. It can't be long and complicated—it needs to be succinct and easy to digest. The reason this is the equivalent of an A is because by sending notice 48 hours in advance, providing a new (specific) deadline and a very brief rationale, you're demonstrating all the right skills: being organized, good communication, good time management. Also you're avoiding surprises.

Surprises are your enemy. Never surprise your boss.

Leave work early

Don't make the mistake of thinking that if you work late people will think you're a hard worker.

If you work late, people will think you're behind, you can't keep up, you're overwhelmed, you don't have a life, you're late on a project—in short, you're not good at your job.

Get your work done. Ask if your boss needs anything else from you. Leave early.

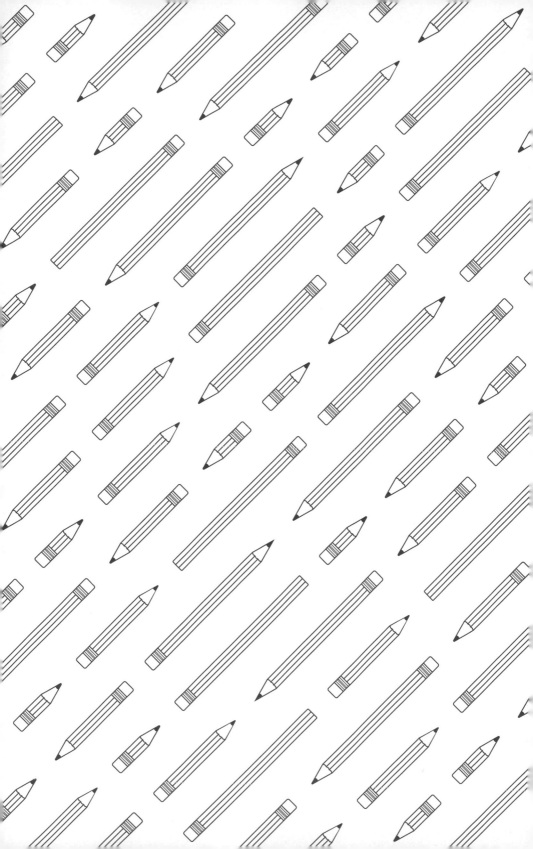

Bonus: Meet weekly

If you're new to a job, it's common for your boss to set a weekly meeting with you—also known as a "touch-base." This is a critical meeting for you. If it isn't happening, ask for it. In fact, demand it.

Without a weekly meeting dedicated to just you and your boss, you have no chance to be successful at your job.

There are three steps to creating a successful weekly meeting:

• Prep before the meeting

• Always send an agenda

• Lead the meeting

Don't get cancelled on
Your weekly meeting with your boss should be a dedicated 30-minute block on the calendar every week. Make sure you pick a time that's not likely to have conflicts.

Best to aim for early morning if possible because if the meeting is scheduled for late afternoon on a Tuesday there's a high likelihood that other meetings will take priority or your boss will be running late and you'll lose your scheduled time with them. This is important to get right.

If your meeting time keeps getting moved, identify and recommend a better time which can become consistent.

Don't schedule on a Monday—there are too many things happening on a Monday. Don't schedule on a Friday—no one likes meetings on a Friday.

Always send an agenda
One other pro tip is to make sure you always send your boss an agenda of topics by 5pm the day prior to your weekly meeting.

There are four benefits to this simple effort:

- It ensures that your touch-base won't be cancelled

- It gives your boss a heads up for what you want to discuss and let's them prepare (if necessary)

- It allows you to be organized and action oriented during the meeting

- It impresses your boss

By being consistent with your meeting time and your agenda format, you will start to establish a steady rhythm of communication with your boss. This is a good thing.

Lead the meeting

It's critical that you go into the meeting with the mind frame that it's your meeting to run. You set the agenda, you lead the discussion, you ask the questions, you get the answers.

This is an important distinction versus the common (lazy) approach of expecting your boss to just tell you what to do. And it's the difference between a 12-month promotion cycle and a 24-month death march.

Here are the elements of a successful meeting:

- Take control—lead the discussion

- Bring two printed copies of the agenda—one for you, one for your boss

- Come prepared with specific questions. What exactly do you need an answer on? Have all the facts ready so your boss can make a decision on the spot

- If time allows, give your boss a very brief summary of one or two interesting projects you are working on. Your goal here is to give the impression that you are making things happen—you are working hard—you are a person of action

- End the meeting early whenever possible. Your boss will appreciate having a few minutes back to check their email or relax before the next meeting

Following these steps will create a positive environment where your boss looks forward to their time with you because they know you'll have pertinent questions, be organized, have good information and finish early.

Bonus: Your boss is not a mind reader

This section can change the trajectory of your career instantly. I'm just warning you.

Tell me if this sounds familiar:

You are doing your work. You are hitting your deadlines. You are generally getting things done—but for some reason it doesn't seem like you are getting credit for all the work you're doing.

Your boss keeps asking you to do things and you do them. Mission accomplished, right?

Wrong.

The truth is, it's not as simple as just completing the work. It's everything that happens before and during the process of doing the work that ultimately influences people's perception of your ability to get things done. To use the common phrase: *The journey is as important as the destination.*

And the thing is, most people work their entire lives never understanding this. That's why I want to take the time to articulate this problem more clearly and then show you how to solve it.

The problem

Here is a common example of what people think happens on a project:

1   Your boss asks you to do something

2   You go away and do it

3   You present it back to your boss

Here is what actually happens on a project:

1   Your boss asks you to do something

2   You go away and work on it

3   Your boss asks you if you are working on the project

4   You say you are working on it

5   A few hours or days later your boss asks again if you are going to be ready for the deadline

6   You say yes

7   You present the project to your boss

Do you see the difference? I hope it's obvious. Most people make the mistake of not considering the importance of their boss' experience of how the project got completed.

Think of it this way: each time your boss asks you if you are working on the project what they are really saying is:

I don't trust you. I'm feeling anxious because I haven't heard from you and I'm worried that the work won't get done.

In this example, because the project required multiple inquiries from your boss, their experience of the project was that it never would have been finished if they hadn't followed up with you, and it was only their inquiries that made the project actually get completed on time.

So your boss may walk away from the project and feel like they did all the work—not you.

And the thing is, you very well may have been on top of every aspect of the project but the fact that your boss asked you instead of you telling them—that's the difference between getting credit for a project and building trust versus getting no credit and being perceived as unreliable.

How to fix the problem

1   Your boss asks you to do something

2   You send your boss a quick email by EOD with an outline
     of how you will accomplish the project and the key
     (specific) timelines you will work toward, including
     check-in points

3   You work on the project

4   You give your boss an update during your weekly touch-
     base meetings or you send a quick status email saying
     everything is on schedule. Keep reminding them of the
     timeline you had agreed to earlier. It's usually best just to
     forward that original email with a quick comment

5   You send an email by 5pm the day before the presentation
     titled **Pre-Read: Project X**. It says: *Hey Boss, here's a pre-read
     of the final presentation. Looking forward to tomorrow*

6   You give the presentation

There is no magic here. It's just a matter of taking a few minutes
to give your boss an update every now and then.

Don't talk yourself into believing that it's better to not bother
your boss with an update and instead just try and get the
project done with no noise. As a manager, I'd much rather get
updates versus chasing after people like a babysitter.

Bonus: How to be the go-to person

One of your goals when you are just getting started should be to find little ways to contribute beyond your immediate job description. Often this can mean doing things that other people don't want to do. Here are two really easy ways to establish yourself as a go-to resource within your team:

Reply quickly
Reply to emails or questions as fast as possible. Being fast with replies is a sure-fire way to build momentum and a good first impression.

But let's be clear: being fast doesn't come before being accurate. Being fast means that you reply within the hour or certainly within the day—it doesn't mean that you send a half complete email one minute after a request.

Pay particular attention to people outside your department or division who are asking for information. These ad hoc requests have a way of being ignored or deprioritized in the flow of daily work because they aren't business critical. If you can establish yourself as someone who replies quickly and accurately to random requests you will start to place yourself at the center of the workflow even though your job title might not show you as a critical member of the team.

One email is better than five

Your boss is busy. One way you can offer to help is to volunteer to pull everyone's information together and send the compiled list. Your boss will appreciate receiving one email with all the division's information instead of needing to compile and chase five separate streams of information themselves.

This may seem granular, but by compiling everyone's information into one spreadsheet you'll get to send the email to your boss for that project. Your name will start to be associated with delivering the work—even though everyone contributed equally.

In fact, the person that sends the email often gets an outsized credit as the leader who delivered the work. Try it and see what happens. Likely your boss will start going directly to you to pull information together for projects. Boom. You're a leader.

1/
How to give a presentation

Let's face it, most of our days in corporate America are spent at a desk looking at a screen—usually Excel spreadsheets or Outlook emails.

It's during presentations that you're given the rare opportunity to step out from the faceless mechanics of being a cog in the wheel and present your best self to your peers and a wider audience.

When Winston Churchill needed to inspire a nation he didn't do it by telegram—he did it by putting himself in front of people and speaking.

Whether you're a CEO or entry-level assistant, being organized in your thoughts and delivery will help your message land with the most impact—and ensure the best audience recall.

What follows is a step-by-step process for creating clear structure and great content that will set you up for success in any presentation.

The perfect structure

Some people are naturally more comfortable speaking in large groups but this doesn't necessarily make them good presenters. Being a good presenter in the business world is a learned skill but even without a ton of experience you can still deliver a great presentation if you set and stick to a clear structure.

This is the exact structure of an effective presentation:

1   The one-sentence overview

2   Explain the structure

3   Headlines

4   Present each topic

5   Tell them what's next

6   The one-sentence conclusion

Using this six-point structure will help you in your prep and memorization. It keeps you organized and also keeps the audience clear on what you're saying.

So let's look at a sample presentation based on this structure. I'm using an example from apparel retailing but this structure is applicable to any topic in any setting.

1. The one-sentence overview

"I am here to present the Boys' Winter Outerwear Collection."

Tell them what you're going to tell them.

2. Explain the structure

"There are three main points I want to discuss."

Let your audience know exactly how many points they should listen for.

You are helping them to structure their note-taking and giving them a guide to how long the presentation will be. You are saying *I am organized—therefore, listen up.*

3. Headlines

"I want to talk about nylon fabrication, length and price points."

Announce the three big headlines you're going to talk about.

One of the main mistakes you want to avoid is making people struggle to follow what you're saying or have to search for your key facts. When you give your audience clear topics with headlines you are practically writing their notes for them. This is a good thing.

4. Present each topic

"The first thing I want to talk about is nylon fabrication. Nylon fabrication is the biggest trend in the market and I see an opportunity for us to..."

"...OK, so that's why I think nylon fabrication is going to be really important for us next season."

You're now ready to present your first topic. Every topic you cover should follow the same pattern: cue, present, summarize. Cue your audience that you're starting a topic. Then cover the topic. Then summarize what you just covered.

The repetition at the beginning and end of each topic might seem unnecessary but your audience will appreciate these organizing cues.

5. Tell them what's next

"OK, we've talked about nylon fabrication so now I want to talk about length. I think we have five minutes left for this last topic."

You want to keep reinforcing your structure throughout.

Don't overlook the importance of letting people know how much longer the presentation is going to be. This helps people relax. They don't have to worry about time and can focus instead on what you're saying.

Think of all the times you've listened to someone and thought *OH MY GOSH—how long is this person going to talk?* Your only recourse is to guess how many pages of notes they have left in their hands. You become consumed with worry about whether you'll be finished in time to go to the next meeting—or your lunch date—all of which means you haven't been paying attention to a single word for the last five minutes of the presentation.

6. The one-sentence conclusion

"OK, so we have talked about nylon fabrication, why we're going to add longer-length jackets and opportunities to raise price points—does anyone have any questions?"

Remind them what you've told them in one sentence. Open the floor for questions. You're done.

Filling in the blanks

So you've got the structure of a great presentation covered. Now you need to make sure the content of the presentation is just as good—and just as simple. Think of the structure as fixed before you even start—you just need to fill in the blanks.

There are three important aspects of content I want to cover:

• Conclusions

• Hero facts

• Action steps

Jump to conclusions

When you present a topic, you should always state your conclusion first.

Time is limited during presentations and usually everything is running late or the first presenter took up too much time so it's best to get right to the point. You don't want your audience guessing. People want to know where they are going so let them know right away.

Starting with your conclusion can be quite an adjustment. In school we're taught at a very young age to structure our papers with an introduction, supporting evidence and then a conclusion and summary. In the business world it's the exact opposite. Start with the conclusion, and then offer supporting evidence.

If you've done your job well—prepped people before the meeting, set a clear structure for your information and picked the right hero fact—you should be able to move quickly with very few questions.

Hero facts

Getting people's attention and creating recall are key to delivering a good presentation. It isn't a single number or a single fact that matters—it's the way you construct them and the story you tell that takes them from good facts to hero facts.

One of the things you'll quickly discover in the business world is that there's so much data available that you have nearly unlimited numbers to support your argument. Which do you choose?

Should you use numbers, percentages, average weekly sales, total monthly sales, sell-through percentages, gross margin?

It's easy to make a laundry list of numbers and throw them at someone—but no one likes that. And just as importantly, no one remembers that.

My quick rule of thumb is that if you can't memorize the number then it's probably too complicated—and you shouldn't use it.

At its most basic level this challenges you to think: Should you say 265,321 units or should you say 265,000 units?

Or, depending on the context of the number in the bigger picture, should you say about 300,000 units?

When you're building a hero fact I recommend asking yourself the following: *If I could only use one number to prove my point— what would it be?* Equally important to picking the right number is setting the context in which that number exists.

For example, if I tell you *I sold 65,000 units* of a jacket last year, that sounds like a lot right?

Well, it depends.

- What if I tell you *I sold 65,000 units of a jacket but we bought over 300,000 units.* That sounds like it sucks because we only sold 20 percent of the total inventory.

- What if I tell you *I sold 65,000 units of this jacket, which was actually less than 1 percent of the total sales for the outerwear division.* Again, it just went from awesome to who cares simply by adding context.

- What if I tell you *I sold 65,000 units which is more than double the number of jackets my number two competitor sold during the same time period.* All of a sudden the same number is awesome again.

Context is everything. So make sure when you are picking your facts that you are giving them the context they need to support the story you want to tell.

Action steps

Don't just say stuff.

Always, always have action steps. It's just as important as using the right facts and figures.

If something is going wrong, don't just say it's going wrong— say what you're going to do about it. If something is going well, don't just brag about it—you better have an action step associated with it.

Make sure that you don't just present an idea and leave it for others to interpret or be left wondering what the point is. You want to lead the discussion and, by recommending your action step, bring the entire presentation to a point and get an answer so everyone can move forward.

You'll see when we get to the section on how to write an email, I encourage you to use the words **action step** and highlight in bold and red so everyone is clear that things are happening— and better, that you're making things happen.

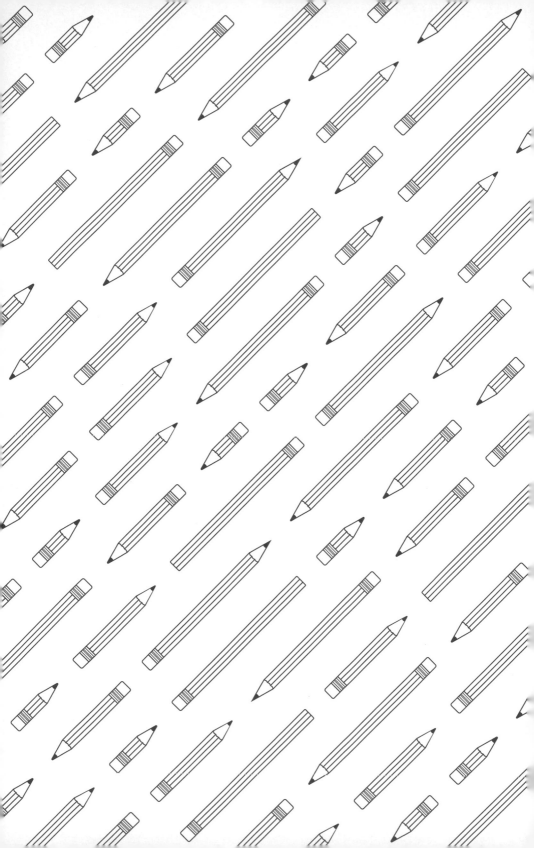

Bonus: I don't know and that's OK (because I'll find out and follow up quickly)

It's OK to not know the answer.

Rather than hem and haw, it is best to simply say *I don't know the answer to that right now but I'll look into it and get back to you right away.*

The key being that you get back to them quickly as promised— meaning by EOD or at latest within 24 hours. Also be sure to cc all relevant members of the group in your reply so that they see your follow-up skills and you get credit for being organized and reliable.

Bonus: Appearances matter

No, I'm not talking about how you dress. Far be it from me to advise you on what to wear to work. I've been wearing Converse and Levi's jeans and Gap white T-shirts to work every day for 15 years. Oh—and now I wear UNIQLO socks and UNIQLO cashmere sweaters. Just FYI...

What I'm talking about is how the information you are presenting is organized and how it looks.

In my case, working in apparel retail, it can mean making sure all the samples are on the same types of hangers. Are they arranged in straight lines? Have I put the most important items at the beginning? Do I have the best color at the front? Are the clothes organized in the same order that my presentation is organized?

This has a direct and significant impact on people's perceptions of you and your presentation.

The same rules apply to handouts. I usually like to advise against handouts unless you have a very number-intensive presentation. The reason being that the minute you give people something to look at you no longer control their attention—or the flow of information. But, if you must use handouts make sure they are organized, simple and easy to follow.

The most basic question you want to ask yourself is—am I organized?

Point being, you want to remove all reasons for distraction so that people are actually listening to what you're saying. Making sure that your words, your actions and your appearance are all saying the same thing will create a powerful harmony in the listener's experience of your presentation.

Bonus: Practice makes perfect

Practice. Practice. Practice.

Malcolm Gladwell tells us it takes 10,000 hours of practice to become the best at something. So if practice makes perfect why not practice more?

Too busy? You'd rather sleep in for 10 minutes in the morning? Your parents made you practice piano so now you hate practicing anything?

Setting personal issues and lame excuses aside, let's talk about a concrete way you can get yourself as much practice as possible—as quickly as possible and as often as possible.

And just to be clear, I'm not talking about practicing one hour before your presentation. That's not practice—that's panic.

When I talk about practice, I mean standing in front of a group—it can even be just one person—and actually speaking out loud.

In a normal business setting you might get to make a presentation to a small group of your colleagues once a week. After that, the frequency of presenting to a group becomes more sporadic. If you're entry level it may even be non-existent.

This is dangerous because it means your opportunities to present—your opportunities to practice standing in front of other human beings and relaying information effectively—will be limited to at most 50 times in an entire year. This is not an impressive number—especially for Mr. Gladwell.

So here's what I recommend you do: find a friend, find a colleague, and in the absence of either of these, find the admin. Ask them if you can have 15 minutes of their time, once a week, and you will stand in front of them and give a presentation.

The physical act of standing is important because you will feel more exposed. It doesn't matter what the topic is—it only matters that you are standing in front of someone and speaking words out of your mouth.

By making practice a priority and following this simple approach you can instantly double, triple or even quadruple the number of presentations you give in your first year. Advantage: you.

2/
How to write an email

Ahh... email. Email, email, email.

Email is the single most important means of communication in corporate America, period. Yes. I said it.

Presentations are good and all, but if you think you are going to change people's opinions or get a key decision made by being a passionate and articulate presenter you will quickly become frustrated and ineffective because presentations to key decision-makers don't happen very often—especially when compared to the amount of information transfer that takes place day-to-day and hour-by-hour through email.

Plus, unlike presentations, with email you don't have to wait for someone else to schedule it. You can do it anytime you want. Emails are so common, so everyday, most people don't even think about whether what they're sending is good or not—they just send it. They click reply and basically puke their thoughts onto the keyboard.

It's a shame because so much value is lost through ineffective emails. Teams and entire organizations waste a huge amount of time—probably thousands of hours per week—asking follow-up questions, waiting for follow-up answers to the follow-up questions and asking follow-up questions to the follow-up answer to the original follow-up question.

Pull up your inbox and scan it for the number of replies to a single email.

It probably started simply enough. You wanted to tell everyone that their recap was due by Friday. But then you didn't attach the format so someone had to ask you how to submit the information. Someone else wasn't clear if it was due Friday or EOD Friday. Someone else wasn't sure how they should even find the information to recap. All of a sudden your original email has a bunch of replies over two days and no actual work has even been accomplished.

I'm here to help.

Eight requirements of an awesome email

The rules of good communication are the same whether you're standing in front of 100 people, talking one-on-one with your boss or using this crazy thing called email.

To start, follow the same rules laid out in the presentation section. This means start with your conclusion and follow with your supporting hero facts. But with that common foundation in place, you now need to follow specific rules to maximize the effectiveness of your emails.

Here are the eight requirements of an awesome email:

1   Subject

2   Deadlines

3   Highlights

4   Bullet points

5   Above the fold/Below the fold

6   Room to breathe

7   The attachment trap

8   The attachment trap part 2

1. Subject

Make sure your subject line is specific, punchy and action oriented: **Jeans Project: Launch Meeting Recap—Action Required**.

2. Deadlines

If there is a deadline in your email, meaning you need someone to do something by a specific time, you must include it in the subject line: **Action Required: Due 4pm Wednesday**. And if you want to be truly best in class, you will be specific with the person's name for the deadline. **Owner: Chris Goble—Deadline: 4pm Wednesday, August 18**.

And while we are here—I might as well tell you that "Due Friday" is not a deadline. Due Friday at 3pm is a deadline. By the same rationale "due EOD" is not a deadline. Due 5pm Wednesday is a deadline. Be specific—otherwise you will find yourself disappointed not to have an answer before you go home.

One trick I like to use is setting a deadline with an off-beat time—**Action Required: Due 4:47pm Wednesday**. By choosing an unusual time for the deadline you will increase the likelihood of your recipient paying attention. After all, it's way more fun to deliver something by 4:47pm on Wednesday than EOD.

3. Highlights

Make sure you always highlight in **bold** (or even red) the deadline within the body of the email.

It is your job to appropriately highlight the key action steps you are requesting. It is not the audience's job to hunt for deadlines or directions within a long email.

4. Bullet points

Always use bullet points.

- Don't use a dash (-)

- Don't use an asterisk (*)

- Don't use an underscore (_)

- Don't indent because depending on the size of the screen each recipient uses to read your email the formatting will look completely different.

- Bullet points have the benefit of being a physical marker of separation no matter the reader's device.

- Bullet points should be limited to one or two sentences.

- Bullet points project *I am organized—therefore, pay attention to what I am telling you.* This is a good thing.

5. Above the fold/Below the fold

In the news world a key measure of value is not just whether you are on the front page but whether you are above the fold or below the fold—meaning either you are part of the headlines that everyone sees on first impression at the newsstand or someone had to pick up the paper, flip it over and then see your article.

In the digital world the same principle applies to the home page. What can the reader see when they first go to the website without scrolling down? This is where the essential information has to be placed. Same for an email.

You have to get all of your key points (conclusion and deadline) above the fold—which means in the first 10 lines of an email. Chances are your boss won't even read below the fold if they don't like what's above the fold.

6. Room to breathe

Formatting an email is as important as the content. If the email itself isn't attractive and well organized people are much more likely to skip the email until later—or miss the point you're trying to make.

Big blocks of text are the enemy and should be avoided at all costs.

An often overlooked but effective trick is to give the email content room to breathe. How? Just skip a space between each bullet point. Sometimes this can be at odds with the above-the-fold strategy, but you'll find the balance.

7. The attachment trap

Never send an email with no content and expect everyone to click on the attachment. In fact, you should assume that no one will open the attachment—therefore it's up to you to provide a succinct summary of the point you want to make.

Treat the attachment merely as supporting evidence. No one should even need to open it since you've provided a summary for the recipient to easily understand. This is especially true in a mobile world where opening an attachment is still inconvenient on your mobile device.

8. The attachment trap part 2

If you send an attachment you better have it formatted to print. Not formatting to print is a super effective way to make everyone hate you.

One more pro tip:

The goal is no questions. When you send out an email pay attention to the questions you get in reply. More often than not the questions will highlight to you a key piece of information that you neglected to include. Learn from this—and set a goal to eliminate replies and questions for emails you send. This will ultimately save time for everyone.

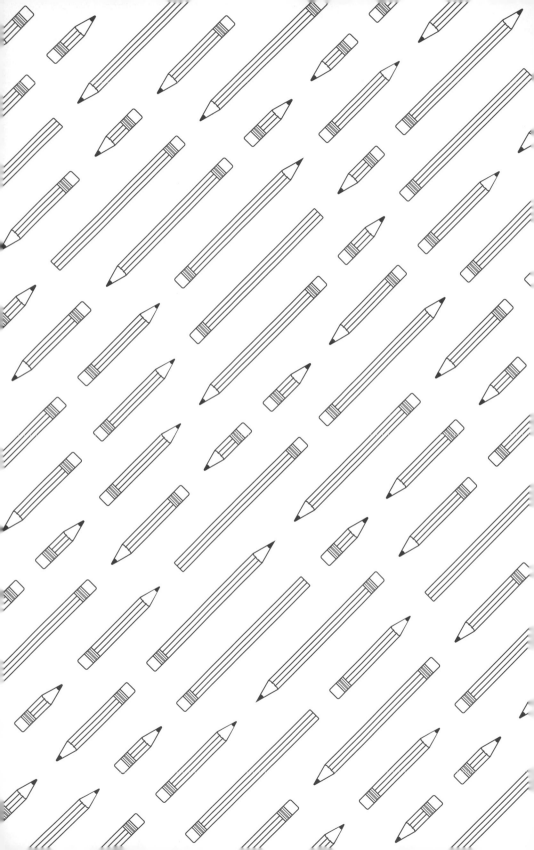

Bonus: What's black and white and read all over?

Emails have the potential to do more harm than good.

They can reach wide audiences, many of whom you may not have originally intended to read your message. Free of context, tone and personal intimacy, emails can be manipulated, framed and used against you.

If you write a bad email—use the wrong language, talk about something or someone in the wrong way—best of luck walking that back. The email will take on a life of its own, possibly landing in the wrong person's inbox and landing you an invitation to HR.

On the flip side, if you are writing good emails and presenting yourself in an effective way, your message can travel to people within the organization to whom you would never normally have access. Your email becomes your ambassador to the upper echelons of management.

So take a step back and consider whether you are spending enough time making sure every email, like every presentation, is representing you in an effective manner.

Emails may seem transitory but once you hit send they are as good as written in stone.

Bonus: Power of the pre-read

The pre-read is your secret weapon.

No one will see you do it, your boss may not even consciously register it, but it's the fast track to an early promotion and a great relationship with your boss. Providing a pre-read instantly achieves the most essential requirements of a successful reputation at work: trust, organization, teamwork, clarity and delivering work early.

In its most basic sense a pre-read is exactly what it sounds like: a chance for stakeholders to preview a document before it is shared more widely through email or the final presentation.

What is the point of the pre-read?

- It shows your boss that you are organized and ahead of schedule

- It gives your boss a chance to absorb your presentation on their own time and at their own pace, creating an environment where deeper thought and insights can be found

- It makes your boss feel like a VIP—they're getting a sneak preview

- If there's something controversial, it gives your boss an opportunity to provide feedback prior to the presentation so you can make an adjustment

- Your boss gets a soft copy version of the presentation which makes it easy for them to forward to their boss or others within the organization. This helps your name travel within the company tied to a project of which you're presumably proud

How do I send a pre-read?

Often this takes the form of simply sending a quick email titled **PRE-READ: Project X** with a simple note:

Hi Boss, just wanted to shoot over a quick pre-read of the big presentation tomorrow.

It's all pretty straightforward as we have discussed but I think page seven is going to be the hot topic around shifting our price points within the category. I've tried to capture the competitive landscape and the GM implications, but let me know if you have any specific feedback on how best to approach.

When sending a pre-read with an attachment, always print out the attachment and leave it on your boss' desk with a post-it note: *Per my email today: pre-read for tomorrow's meeting.*

This has four clear benefits:

- You get credit twice—for the email and for the physical copy

- You've made life easy for your boss and they'll appreciate that

- You've made sure that your pre-read won't get lost in the email shuffle of day-to-day work

- You've created a high level of engagement with your boss and higher probability for some constructive feedback that will improve your presentation tomorrow

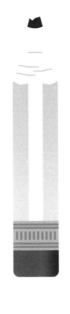

3/
How to get promoted

Better title. More money. Better office. Make Dad happy. We all have our reasons for wanting to get promoted, but most people don't know how to make it happen.

Sure, in some rare cases you'll be promoted at the exact moment when you really deserve it—but in reality you're just as likely to be promoted for being in the right place at the right time. Likewise you may get passed over because of circumstances out of your control despite really deserving a promotion.

The purpose of this chapter is to move you from a passive participant in the process of your promotion into an active driver who is in charge of setting the timeline and ensuring your promotion.

There are a lot of things that go into being promoted which most people don't understand but if you can focus on these three key elements you'll have a better chance than most.

- Setting your goals

- Understanding the playing field

- Making your case

Setting your goals

The first step to getting promoted is setting your goals.

Believe me, it's not as easy as it sounds and most people get it wrong right from the start. In fact, most people don't even believe in the importance of setting goals. They are so anxious to get promoted that they see the goal-setting process as a nuisance keeping them from doing the actual work that will get them promoted. They are wrong.

It's like saying you are going to drive cross country from San Francisco to New York City but you didn't have time to look up directions because you didn't want to be late.

Think of your goals as having the same importance as those directions. Write good goals or you'll end up wasting a lot of time and energy.

Here are nine specific ways to set goals that will help you get promoted quickly:

1	Don't cut and paste

2	Be specific

3	Don't write one-year goals

4	Build skills with one-month goals

5	I love three-month goals (and you should too)

6	Doing your job won't get you promoted

7	Make your goals measurable

8	Tell them you want to be promoted

9	Pick a day, any day

1. Don't cut and paste

Usually hand-me-down goals will be generic, broad and unspecific to you and your individual development. Most often they take the form of four big goals, three of which will be based on total division results with the fourth—window dressing—being an individual goal you're asked to write yourself.

To be clear, this type of generic goal-setting does nothing for your personal development.

More often than not it's a comically corporate process where you fill out a goals form around midyear (when half your work is already behind you) and then you don't talk about, think about or touch your goals until HR sends a reminder to fill out the goals form at the end of the year.

This is corporate eyewash. It serves no real purpose other than reassuring everyone involved that they are doing what they are supposed to be doing. If you're asked to fill out the form go ahead and do it—but you must also separately write up your personal goals and present them to your manager.

2. Be specific

Be very specific.

You aren't going to improve your financial skills—you are going to set a one-hour meeting every week with your financial planner to study your monthly forecast.

You aren't going to improve cross functional relationships— you are going to set weekly one-on-one meetings with all of your key functional partners and solicit feedback from the team at 3, 6 and 12-month periods to measure improvement.

You aren't going to beat plan—you are going to rate your performance down to specific percentages: A = 5 percent over plan; B = 0 to 4.9 percent over plan; C = anything under plan.

3. Don't write one-year goals

Too much can change in 365 days within a corporate organization to make this a reliable time frame. Yes, one could also argue that nothing changes in 365 days in corporate America but that's a different topic for a different day.

Writing your goals with only an eye toward the year-end review is a mistake because what you will end up with are broad, generic goals which won't be useful as guides to your day-to-day work and behavior.

Stick to goals with shorter time frames where results are easier to measure.

4. Build skills with one-month goals

If you set a goal for one month it's much easier to measure and achieve. You have just four weeks to accomplish it so it's easy to break down the steps and measure the results.

If you set monthly goals for an entire year you will have acquired 12 new measurable skills. This process should never end during your entire career.

Now compare this to your current process of development in which you measure the number of years you've been in a position as reflective of how your skills are improving.

How many times have you heard someone say *I just feel like I'm not learning anything new?*

There is always another skill for you to master and by committing to a process of learning one new skill per month—no matter how small—you will quickly stockpile these small arms into a powerful arsenal. Multiply this by a few years and wow—hello, Mr. President.

5. I love three-month goals (and you should too)

Three months is the optimal length of time to measure a mean-ingful goal. While one-month goals quietly stockpile small skills which are useful in hand-to-hand combat, three-month goals will be noticeable achievements that can directly help you get promoted.

These are the types of goals that will be the most compelling when you're writing your end-of-year summary of accomplish-ments. I like to call them flagship accomplishments.

6. Doing your job won't get you promoted

When anyone that works for me tells me they want to get promoted in the next year the first thing I tell them is that they have to get all the basics right: be on time, deliver early and accurate work and play well with others. This is the cost of entry.

The second thing I tell them is they need to undertake at least two flagship accomplishments in the next six months. This means they need to create and accomplish at least two high-visibility, high-recall projects that everyone can agree went above and beyond day-to-day normal responsibilities. This can be leading a project across multiple functions, recommending a new business strategy for growth or initiating after-work charity hours.

The truth is it can be anything—but it has to be clear what you did. It has to have instant recall for everyone across the organization so that when your boss is trying to convince someone about your promotion at the end of the year, they have two or three easy, high-visibility talking points that no one is going to dispute.

Many times your boss' boss won't even know who you are so these flagship accomplishments act as your calling card. *Which one is he again? Oh, he's the one that led our back-to-school strategy and he also started our program of volunteering at the elementary school.* Right—now you're someone.

7. Make your goals measurable

There is a big difference between telling your boss *I worked really hard* versus *I beat plan by 25 percent, I scheduled and led weekly cross-functional meetings and our survey scores for store satisfaction increased 10 percent over last year.*

Being specific and writing quantifiable goals is essential to moving the judgment of your performance from emotional to factual during your final year-end review.

8. Tell them you want to be promoted

Managers aren't mind readers. You need to make sure your boss knows you want to be promoted. Do not make lame excuses about being modest. You need to get past any discomfort in bringing up the topic because it is completely unrealistic to think you will be promoted if you and your boss have not talked about it at least four times over the past year.

9. Pick a day, any day

Just as important as broaching the topic of your promotion is being specific with your boss about the timeline for your promotion.

Of course your boss will never guarantee you a promotion on a certain day but you should at least align on a general sense of timing—12 months, 18 months, etc. Usually promotions are handed out at year-end or midyear so use these already exist-ing milestones as a starting place, and partner with your boss to get as specific as possible—hopefully to the month level.

Setting a time frame is important to ensuring you and your boss have the same perception of your current performance and potential for promotion. If you go into the discussion thinking you are ready for a promotion now and your boss says 18 months—well, you have some self-evaluation to do but at least now you know what the expectations are.

Understanding the playing field

The second step in building your case for promotion is to understand who the key decision makers are. You need to ask yourself *Who's Who and Who Am I?* Without understanding the landscape of the organization you're way more likely to drift into the promotion slow lane.

A lot more than merit determines who gets promoted and when. Once you understand this you'll have a greater appreciation for how difficult it is to get promoted and how much work it takes above and beyond your day-to-day job.

There arc four key players for you to be aware of:

- Your boss' boss

- Peers

- HR

- Your boss

Your boss' boss

It's not just your boss who is deciding if you are getting promoted. It is your boss' boss, your boss' boss' boss plus a few higher-level people from other functions and divisions who you've probably never even heard of.

This doesn't mean you should start trying to impress the higher-ups—that's a rookie move. Trying to go over your boss' head is a fast track to the slow promotion lane.

Your job is to go out of your way to make your boss look good. Make no mistake, without your boss' firm endorsement and support a faster-than-usual promotion is not going to happen. One more thing related to this topic of bosses and boss' bosses—does everyone know your name?

Anonymity is the enemy of promotion. If no one outside your immediate team knows who you are, it's a problem. Make sure that people know who you are. This is why I recommend you set at least two one-on-one meetings with your boss' boss during the year.

Peers

Understand that giving promotions is a very political process.

Is there a peer who started the same time as you? If so, this is a problem because you will be compared with each other—and if they are found lacking—sometimes management won't want to promote one of you without promoting the other. They do this simply because they don't want to hurt someone's feelings.

It sounds ridiculous but it's true. This exact scenario happened to me when I was getting promoted from merchant to senior merchant. My boss actually said *You are ready Justin—but Carla isn't ready and we think it will hurt her feelings if you get promoted first.*

There may be someone in another division who is also up for a promotion. In this case, your boss has to convince not just their boss but also their peers that you deserve the promotion— sometimes at the expense of someone else.

The point is, it's bigger than just you.

HR

Now is a good time to talk about your relationship with HR—or lack thereof—because when you're going for a promotion inevitably HR is going to be involved.

I can tell you from experience there are really good HR people and there are really bad HR people—and generally there aren't a lot in between. But no matter where they land on the spectrum of good and bad, you need to have a relationship with them.

I recommend meeting at least four times a year so that you stay familiar, they know who you are, what your situation is and what your goals are. This way, when it comes to promotion time, you'll already be on the radar.

Your boss

If you think you deserve a promotion and you are doing a good job, you are likely not high on your boss' radar of concerns. In fact, your boss probably takes you for granted. You are actually too good. This can be a problem.

They are worried about their own job, they are worried about their own promotion, they are worried about their own peers that just got promoted—especially if they themselves didn't. They are worried about someone else on your team who is taking up all of their attention and they are worried about stuff outside of work.

So, knowing that your boss is busy and knowing that your boss is going to have to make the case for you to be promoted to a bunch of people, your goal is to make it as easy for them as possible. Hopefully you have done this through your everyday performance but, for all the reasons I just mentioned, this isn't enough—now you need to put everything in writing.

Making your case

I recommend you approach each promotion as a trial lawyer, building your case with clear, concise facts, creating a believable timeline and making the jury (your boss and everyone else) feel that it's an easy decision—beyond a reasonable doubt.

There are five stages to making your case for promotion:

1   Summarize your accomplishments

2   Schedule the meeting

3   Give a warning shot

4   Meet

5   Live with the consequences

1. Summarize your accomplishments

The reason that you write clear and measurable goals is so that when you accomplish them no one can dispute your performance.

But equally important to setting and achieving your goals is the physical act of summarizing your accomplishments in an effective way. This is about making sure you get credit for everything you have accomplished.

Notice I said that YOU summarize your goals and end-of-year performance. Most people will make the mistake of leaving the summary of their performance to their boss. This is the equivalent of running the length of the field and stopping on the one-yard line to start celebrating.

Remember everything I just said about how busy your boss is? Remember how they have 99 problems and you aren't one? You need to do the work so your boss doesn't have to.

To start, build your case by summarizing your accomplishments in the best way possible, drawing on everything you learned from the previous chapters about how to give a presentation and how to write an email.

Always start with business results. After that, it's important that you list your two to three flagship accomplishments. Just like normal emails, be succinct—the fewer words, the better for each bullet point. You need headlines backed up with quantifiable facts—be high-level and specific at the same time.

2. Schedule the meeting

The next thing you want to do is schedule the meeting, but because it can be difficult to find time in your boss' busy schedule, I recommend repurposing one of your existing weekly meetings to focus specifically on making the case for your promotion.

Be smart about the timing you set for the meeting. While end-of-year reviews may take place in January, you should be aware that conversations about promotions are likely taking place at the end of November or early December.

It is essential that you have this conversation and, more importantly, provide your boss with the summary of your accomplishments well before they are ever pulled into a meeting to talk about promotions within their team.

This is critical—don't mess it up.

3. Give a warning shot

It's important that your boss knows what is coming. Remember, you never want to surprise your boss—with anything.

In this case, you want to give your boss a chance to digest your accomplishments before being confronted by you in person so the best thing to do is send a simple pre-read email with the subject line: **PROMOTION**.

Write an introduction to set the context:

Hi Boss, I'd like to spend some time talking about next steps for a potential promotion. To that end, I summarized my key accomplishments over the past 12 months below. Look forward to discussing at our next weekly one-on-one meeting.

Be sure you have your bullet point list of accomplishments included in the email. Do not include the list as an attachment. As I mentioned in the chapter "How to write an email," you should assume that most attachments are never opened. All key information should always be in the body of the email itself.

Ideally you will send it two days prior to make sure they have time to read it. The chances of having a constructive conversation during your promotion meeting will increase exponentially by providing your boss with this pre-read summary of your accomplishments.

Conversely, if you don't send the pre-read it will feel like a sneak attack. Your boss won't feel prepared and will instead feel pressured. This is not the environment you want to create for the big discussion.

4. Meet

When it comes to the actual meeting itself, your goal should be to be organized, succinct and not talk too much.

Come to the meeting with two printed copies of your accomplishments—one for your boss and one for you.

Understand that your weekly meetings, your pre-read promotion email and your bullet points have done all the work for you before you walk into the room. If you feel an instinct to make your case, chances are you may have missed a step somewhere along the way.

Unlike the rest of your one-on-one meetings, you want to let your boss do the talking. This is important. You've done the work. Now put the pressure on them by not talking.

Make no mistake, your boss has almost certainly already decided if you are going to be promoted or not. This meeting, in and of itself, is not going to change their mind. It should be approached as a confirmation rather than a request.

Set the tone, frame the conversation briefly and then get out of the way.

At this point one of three things will happen depending on what type of boss you have:

You have an awesome boss
They already confirmed you are getting a promotion with all the key players—their boss, their boss' boss, HR and others—in which case they'll say they don't need you to read each bullet point. They'll tell you everything looks good and they'll take a look at it later. Lucky you.

You have a crappy boss
They'll sigh heavily and then proceed to tell you why you aren't going to get a promotion.

They're not a crappy boss because they didn't promote you. That's your fault.

They're a crappy boss because it never should have gotten this far. Getting promoted shouldn't be a surprise ending. It should be a steady and consistent conversation throughout the year based on the goals you set, the feedback you received and the constructive conversations along the way.

If you aren't getting promoted you should already know it before this meeting even takes place. That's what I mean when I say it never should have gotten this far—and that's why I think you have a crappy boss.

You have a lazy boss
The wild card option—a middle ground for which you need to be prepared because it happens to all of us at one point or another.

Stay positive. The good news is that you have your boss' support. The bad news is that your boss kind of sucks.

Your boss has made up their mind that they want to promote you—but they haven't been doing the work to lay the foundation with their boss and HR and now they are realizing it. In this case, they will want to review your list of key accomplishments to see if there is enough for them to make a compelling case for your promotion.

This isn't an ideal situation but you can still have confidence because you've done the work even though your boss hasn't. You've created an easy-to-digest list of evidence and hopefully you've also had your two one-on-one meetings with your boss' boss and HR—so that even if your boss didn't lay the foundation, you did.

5. Live with the consequences

At this point, you've done everything you can.

If you don't get promoted it's OK. Life goes on.

The good news is that you've put yourself on the to-do list and your boss, HR and even your boss' boss will feel the pressure of having disappointed you. I recommend that you set a meeting with HR and ask for some honest feedback about where you are and why you didn't get promoted. Then start the process again until you get there.

If, on the other hand, you do get promoted—congratulations. You're on your way to the long and deliriously fun stage of middle management.

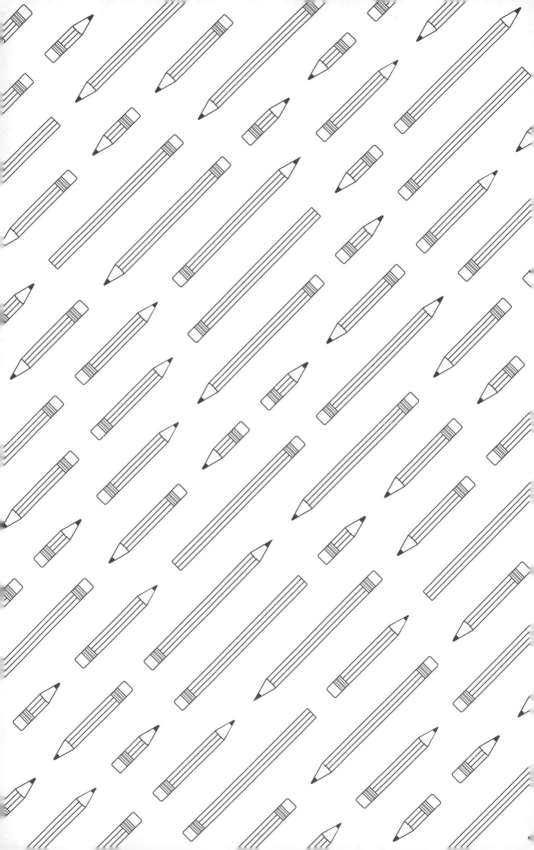

Bonus: How to talk about your promotion without making everyone hate you

Before you close this chapter, we should quickly address how you talk about your desire to be promoted. Here are some guidelines to help you navigate this delicate territory.

Do:
Talk about your desire to be promoted with your boss.

Do:
Set a rough timeline of when you would like to be promoted. Is your goal at midyear, end-of-year, 18 months? The more lead time the better so that your boss won't feel the pressure of an imminent decision. It will also reflect that you're organized and thoughtful and not impatient or unrealistic about your expectations.

Do:
Frame the discussions around your goals and what you're working on. This is a better away of keeping your promotion top of mind without overtly talking about promotion, promotion, promotion.

Do:
Frame your desire for promotion as wanting a chance to have a bigger impact on the business, take on more responsibility, have access to more meetings, learn new skills and have new experiences.

Don't:
Talk about your desire for a title as the motivating factor for your promotion.

Don't:
Compare yourself to weaker co-workers as a justification for your own promotion. Comparing yourself to others will result in a long and unhappy life.

Don't:
Bring up your desire for a promotion more than once a month. This is annoying and will turn people off. If you bring up your desire to be promoted too much it will give the impression that all you care about is the promotion—not the success of the business or the team. You will look selfish. Not a good look for those wanting to be promoted.

Bonus: Save everything

Your memory is not as good as you think it is and there's a good chance you won't remember everything you accomplished over the course of a full year. What happened in February will be a distant memory by December—not just for you but for your boss as well.

You want to make sure you get full credit for your efforts throughout the year so your case for promotion is strong. The easy solution is to create an accomplishments folder in your email.

Get in the habit of stashing emails in the folder to help jog your memory when you sit down to write your end-of-year summary. Save everything. Compliments from your boss, project kick-off emails, business results—everything counts when it comes to building the case for your promotion.

Afterword

It's doubtful they are going to list the speed of your promotion or the results of last quarter on your tombstone.

The truth is none of this stuff matters except if it matters to you. The people, the laughs, the skills you learn—those are the things you'll take with you for the rest of your life.

I wrote this book because I love teaching. I wrote this book because I love seeing people get promoted and because I love seeing people achieve things they never thought themselves capable of.

I hope this book helps you make the most of your effort, time and talent for however long you choose to share it with corporate America. But do me a favor and keep your eye on the prize   yourself, your family, your friends.

Life is short. You should be enjoying it.

Go eat lunch outside.

This book is dedicated to
my first boss—Chris Funk.

Rest in peace.

Justin is currently the UNIQLO USA Chief Merchandising Officer and Director of Brand Marketing. He is also the founder of Black Sheep Postal Service. You can check out what Justin is up to on Instagram @jdkjdkjdkjdk.

Justin has written 14 other books:

Follow Me
Girls Rule
Survival Guide to Urban Beekeeping
The Blacks
Plug
A List of Everything I Like About People From Florida
Marco and the Zombies
18 Fashion Facts
Photobooth
My Wife is _____.
I _____ my husband.
You are not allowed to.
Black Sheep Postal Service – The First Six Months
(Nothing to See Here)
In the Event of My Death

Colophon

#howtowriteanemail

How to write an email
A survival guide to corporate America
Justin Kerr

ECP/004

Art Direction/Design: Boon
boondesign.com

Editing: Marc Weidenbaum

Copy Editing: Eric Searleman

Illustration: Zac Oransky

Print Advisor: Celeste McMullin

Typography: Graphik, Tiempos

Printed by Regal Printing Limited in HK

First Edition: 500

ISBN: 978-0-9898320-2-1

ExtraCurricular Press
extracurricularpress.com

This and other ExtraCurricular Press
printed matter can be ordered direct
from the publisher:
extracurricularpress.com

Watch out for the next installment of Justin Kerr's survival guide to corporate America:

How to be a boss